PIANO / VOCAL / GUITAR

TOP COUNTRY
OF '06-'07

ISBN-13: 978-1-4234-2555-7
ISBN-10: 1-4234-2555-3

HAL•LEONARD®
CORPORATION
7777 W. BLUEMOUND RD. P.O. BOX 13819 MILWAUKEE, WI 53213

Visit Hal Leonard Online at
www.halleonard.com

ALYSSA LIES

Words and Music by
JASON MICHAEL CARROLL

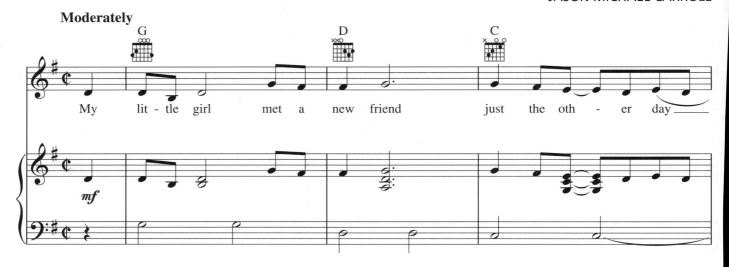

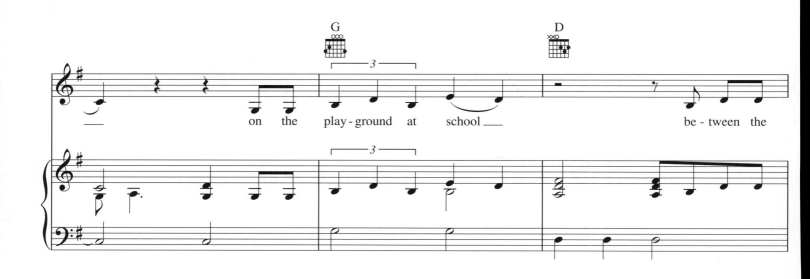

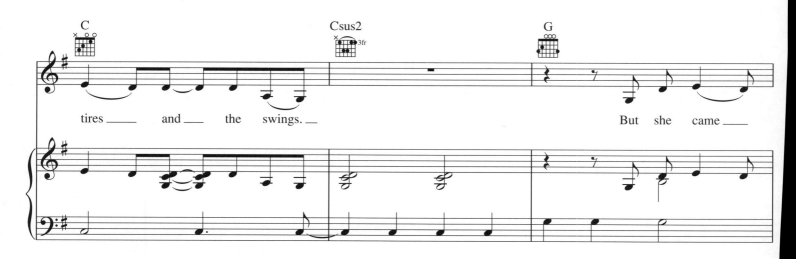

BEFORE HE CHEATS

Words and Music by JOSH KEAR
and CHRIS TOMPKINS

Steady Country Swing-Rock

Right now he's prob-'ly slow danc-ing with a bleach-blonde tramp and she's
Right now, she's prob-'ly up sing-ing some white trash ver-sion of Sha-

prob-'ly get-ting frisk-y. Right now, he's prob-'ly buy-ing her some
ni a ka-ra-o-ke. Right now, she's prob-'ly say-ing, "I'm drunk"

A GOOD MAN

Words and Music by VICTORIA SHAW,
ADRIENNE FOLLESE and KEITH FOLLESE

* *Recorded a half step lower.*

CRASH HERE TONIGHT

Words and Music by
TOBY KEITH

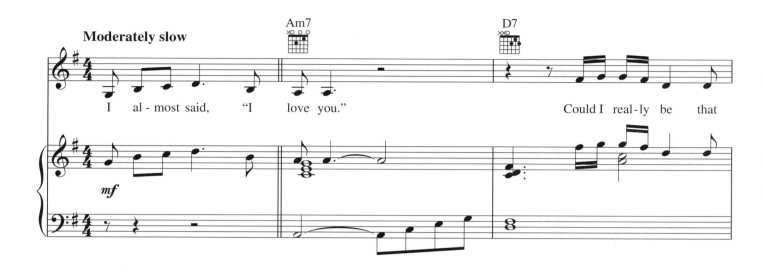

I al-most said, "I love you." Could I real-ly be that

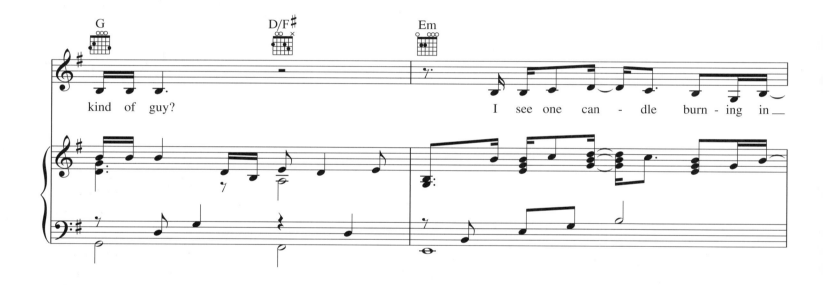

kind of guy? I see one can-dle burn-ing in

your eye and watch my heart fill up

EVERY MILE A MEMORY

Words and Music by STEVE BOGARD,
BRETT BEAVERS and DIERKS BENTLEY

I LOVED HER FIRST

Words and Music by WALT ALDRIDGE
and ELLIOT PARK

With a light back-beat

Look at the two __ of you, danc-in' that way, __ lost in the mo-ment and each oth-er's face. So much in love, __ you're a-lone __ in this place, like there's no-bod-y else __ in the world. __

LITTLE BIT OF LIFE

Words and Music by TONY MULLINS
and DANNY WELLS

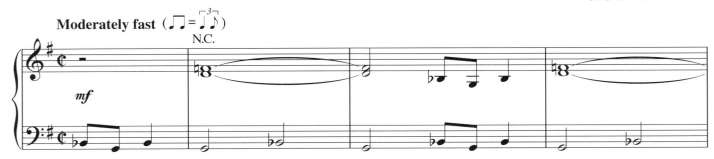

MOUNTAINS

Words and Music by LARRY BOONE,
PAUL NELSON and RICHIE McDONALD

Moderately

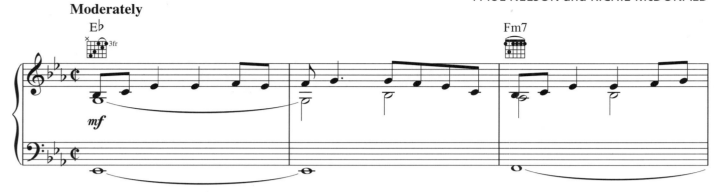

MY LITTLE GIRL
from the Twentieth Century Fox Motion Picture FLICKA

Words and Music by TIM McGRAW
and TOM DOUGLAS

MY, OH MY

Words and Music by JESSICA HARP,
MICHELLE BRANCH, WAYNE KIRKPATRICK
and JOSH LEO

This con-crete road ___ used to
Times have changed ___ and ___

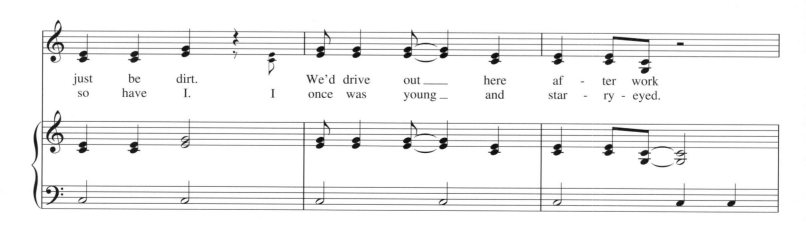

just be dirt. We'd drive out ___ here af-ter work
so have I. I once was young ___ and star-ry-eyed.

MY WISH

Words and Music by STEVE ROBSON
and JEFFREY STEELE

ONE WING IN THE FIRE

Words and Music by BOBBY PINSON
and TRENT TOMLINSON

SHE'S EVERYTHING

Words and Music by BRAD PAISLEY
and WIL NANCE

she's a   yel-low pair of runnin' shoes, a hole-y pair of jeans

she looks great in an-y thing   she's I want a piece of choc-la

great in cheap sun-glass-es she looks

SOME PEOPLE CHANGE

Words and Music by MICHAEL DULANEY,
JASON SELLERS and NEIL THRASHER

TIM McGRAW

Words and Music by TAYLOR SWIFT
and LIZ ROSE

WATCHING YOU

Words and Music by BRIAN GENE WHITE,
RODNEY ATKINS and STEVE DEAN

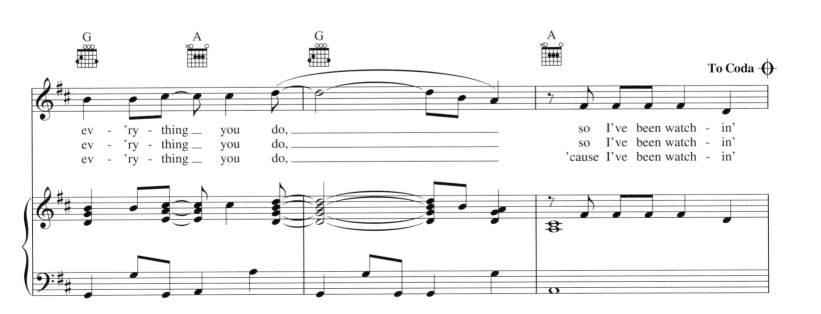

YOU SAVE ME

Words and Music by BRETT JAMES
and TROY VERGES

WANT TO

Words and Music by BOBBY PINSON,
JENNIFER NETTLES and KRISTIAN BUSH

I packed a cool - er and a change of clothes.___ Let's jump in, see___
I got your ring_____ a - round my neck,___ and a cou - ple of nights___

___ how far ___ it _____ goes. _____
___ I don't ___ re - gret. _____